Monica Lewinsky's Guide to Dating

Monica Lewinsky's Guide to Dating

by Anonymous Too

toExcel

San Jose New York Lincoln Shanghai

To Kenneth Starr

In the spirit of forgiveness, may my good wishes
follow you to your eternity in Dante's Eighth Circle.

Contents

Preface

Monica knows the rules of dating. Many people reading the Starr report, watching television network coverage, seeing Monica's interviews, watching MSNBC analysis and CNN analysis and Fox News analysis and CNBC analysis, or reading Monica's book learned that they, on the other hand, did not know the rules of dating, and that is unfair. Everyone should know the same rules.

That is the purpose of this book: to ensure that in this great country of ours, where everyone can aspire to be President, or at least aspire to the President, everyone gets to compete on a level playing field, knowing the same set of rules. The book is about Equality. It's about Opportunity. It's about America at its finest, or, at least, most popular. It was written for the good of mankind, to make this a better world.

This book explains Monica's rules of dating, but Monica is far too busy piecing her shattered life back together and re-establishing her privacy through desperate attendance at award shows, premieres, famous restaurants, book signing tours, interview sessions, and other public events to write page after page of actual sentences herself. The words were put to paper by a well-respected, world-famous psychic who channeled Monica's thoughts. The good professor declines to accept the thanks of the dating-age population (approximately ages 13 through 69) of the country, and prefers to remain anonymous in order to preserve his reputation for dealing with only matters of the most elevated importance.

This great man—let's call him Professor XXX—has a long and distinguished career assisting law enforcement authorities in locating crime scenes and identifying criminals, as well as in establishing the intent of recently-departed dear ones in cases of disputed wills and even in finding lost pets. He is an expert channeler, and used his considerable skills in this area to record the advice in this guide. He reports that the mental communication from Monica was exceptionally clear, free of the usual distractions such as plans, mortgages, bills, philosophy, introspection, regrets, and other daily mental activity that he often finds in peoples' minds and that clutter most such communication. After placing himself in a straight-backed chair in a slightly darkened, quiet room with a flickering television whose volume was turned down to an indistinct, repetitive mumble, Professor XXX de-focused his eyes and focused his mind on Monica. After this intense focus relieved his mind of intelligent thought, he sank into a semi-hypnotic state. In this state, Monica's thoughts came to him unbidden, and perhaps even unbeknownst to Monica herself, as though she were unconsciously speaking to the world through him. Her guidance was recorded, transcribed, and edited to become this volume. The exhausting channeling sessions lasted for hours, with breaks during the dinner hour wherever Monica was. (Taking in protein seemed to interfere with Monica's thought processes.)

The Professor notes that unlike his psychic efforts to assist law enforcement, his efforts in this case seemed to be considerably enhanced with the internal application of measured amounts of eighteen-year-old Scotch. In fact, his assistants noted that Monica's volubility increased in direct proportion to the amounts of Scotch applied—a scientific finding that may lead to more effective psychic support to law enforcement in the future as well as the gathering of information from beyond.

This, then, is the edited transcript of Monica's rules of dating. Like Richard Nixon's edited transcripts, they can present only the most essential elements; they can not re-create the experiences that led to success, loving (albeit limited) relationships, and world fame. But whether your goal is an immediate, intense love affair with a public figure or a long-term, profitable relationship, this volume will bring your dating skills to the very peak of fin-de-siècle social consciousness and intimacy.

"He had a glow about him that was magnetic. He exudes a sexual energy. I thought to myself: 'Now I see what all the girls are talking about'."

—Monica Lewinsky

Stage 1
Choosing the Man

The very first thing to do in your search for love and self-respect is to choose a man.

I've been through this—a couple of times—and you can learn from just sitting and reading this book what I had to learn in other positions. It won't do to pick just any man. You need to pick the right man, and I'm here to help you do it. There are only a few things to look for in a man. In fact, these three simple things are the most important:

His marital status. I hate to say it, but lots of the stuff your mother told you was wrong. She learned her lessons about life in an earlier time before women were liberated—and dating became a competitive sport. (My mom is a real modern woman, having come through her divorce from a wealthy man with a comfortable settlement, so I don't mean *her* when I talk about advice from mothers. I mean *your* mother.) Just as your mother told you, you *do* have to check a man's marital status, but not for the reasons she gave you. You want to make sure he is *married*.

If you date an unmarried man, you'll eventually have to meet his relatives. Let's face it; do you want to be the kind of girl that a man wants to bring home to his mother? You'd rather be the kind that he shows off to his father. Can you imagine canceling a hair appointment or a shopping trip because Bobby wants you to meet his grandparents? (Grandfather's probably too old to be a candidate for you.) An unmarried man may want to spend way too much time with you. Do you really want some guy hanging around while you're watching the Oscars in your curlers and opening your second bag of Oreos? An unmarried man will expect you to help him in his career. Do you really want to play the pleasant hostess when Bobby brings his old gray-bearded boss home for dinner? Do you want to have to grin and bear it as Bobby's Boss squeezes your fanny as you bend over to check the roast? Of course not. (If you ever *do* find yourself stuck in this situation, perhaps you should check out the boss as he's checking you out.) Unmarried men sometimes get careless and get you pregnant. (Don't believe any claims about childhood mumps making him sterile! That line's been used.) Do you want to go to a hospital and wear one of those awful gowns, or have your abdomen swell up so you can't fit into any stylish clothes? Get *real*. You want a man, but you still want to have a life. So go for a married man. You won't have to make a fuss about his grandma's new teeth, you'll have time to do the things you enjoy, and you won't have all those bothersome obligations.

Another reason to set your sights on a married man is that married men are more appreciative. They know they can count on you, and that is really important to them. In your limited meetings, they know that you will never have a headache. You will always be willing (but see Stage Seven!), and always make them feel like real men. You're not a *wife*. They know that you will never talk about a plugged-up garbage disposal, or a child's grades, or new carpet for the house, or upcoming family reunions for them to attend, or the menu for a dinner party, or the weight of drapery fabrics, or other things that they have to pretend to care about when they are at home. They will always be glad to see you.

You could *start out* with single men, but that's just for practice. (More about "practicing" later.) Be open to possibilities. When you practice on single men, check out their fathers (who are presumably wealthier, with a good chance of being married). How successful is his brother? I've moved from one sibling to another and back again during my training phase, though that does add a new dimension to "sibling rivalry." You should if at all possible keep your single men friends after your practice with them, because they are good contacts for meeting married men. It's also good to bounce ideas off them, because they understand the different times at which times men think with different parts of their bodies. (You can make a pretty good guess at this, especially after some practice, but it helps to have the expert opinion of a male friend who has experienced the numbing effect of having all the blood leave his brain.)

His job. Many loving, charming, sexy men have jobs like plumber, mechanic, drug lord bagman, and pari-mutuel ticket seller. You don't want them. What are you dating for? Love, self-respect, and bragging rights. When you gab with your girlfriends, you want to be able to brag about your lover's job. (The only exception is that you can date a man with *any* job as long as he has a certain remarkable physical feature you can brag about—but it has to be really exceptional, and it has to stand up to comparison with your girl friends' stories.) His job has to command respect. Remember, your self-respect derives from the man who dates you. Sure, the refrigerator repairman may be kind, stable, loving, handsome, muscular, faithful (well, not faithful, because we've already ruled out single men), affluent, and generally wonderful, but do you want to date him? *Anyone* can date him. Do you want to tell your girlfriends "It was remarkable. I was just staring at his butt crack as he fixed my coils, and something happened!" *Please*!

Mr. Right has to have a job that commands respect. Professor, company president, psychic, Governor (except of Minnesota), or, if you are in Washington, D.C., Cabinet Member (except Education), Senator, or above. I left out "Representative" because while there are 435 Representatives, there are only 100 Senators so the law of supply and demand makes a Senator a better catch. (However, you might consider a man with a key leadership position in the House, especially now that Mr. Gingrich is gone.) Ambassadors from first-world countries that export luxury items to the U.S. are possible candidates, but avoid Ambassadors from countries that rent their embassies, are in sweaty climates, or don't give good parties. There is no such thing as setting your sights too high. Even Presidents of the United States are available. I don't just mean the current one. (He's available to anyone, so he almost doesn't count. Linda Tripp tells me that Attorney General isn't the *only* position Janet Reno has had in this Administration.)

Anyway, make sure that he is important, and it will help if he is a public figure so that your girlfriends can see him, and see people making a fuss over him (just as they will see you in the same type of photo with him after you are successful). That shows that he is important, and therefore that you are important. It goes *almost* without saying that he must make enough money that he can afford to show his affection for you with gifts.

Dating a public figure is a good idea for two other reasons. First, it usually limits his opportunity to date other women. He can't pick up women in public places. With this dating guide, you will know how to compete, but it won't hurt to narrow the field of competitors right from the start by picking a man whose opportunities are limited. You don't want someone who meets a lot of women or can date freely. (No airline pilots, please.) Second, it gives him a lot to lose if he doesn't treat you right when you reach the later stages—including the Getting Dumped stage—of your relationship.

His appearance. Even though you won't be parading through Bloomingdale's with your beloved, your girlfriends will see him, because you've picked someone whose photograph appears in newspapers, faculty newsletters, or annual reports. So while he doesn't have to be really handsome, he has to be at least cute. As with most rules, though, there is an exception. If his job is really, really, big, then he can be pudgy and cuddly, or even overweight from eating too many cheeseburgers. He could even be short, old, wrinkled, and speak with a German accent. But it does help if you feel some animal magnetism, some raw attraction. If—no, *when*—you are successful, you will be doing lots of intimate things with your man, and it helps if you don't feel compelled to close your eyes while you do them.

To build your confidence, you may want to start small and work your way up. Instead of starting with a company president, try starting with the Chief Financial Officer, if you don't mind the boredom. (Remember, this is just practice for you. It may not be enjoyable, but it's necessary work. Before you swing for the fences, you need to practice under the stands.) Or you can even start with a junior executive if you absolutely have to. If your area of interest is academia, you don't have to start with a dean. A full (tenured) professor would do nicely, and assistant professors, associate professors, even starting at the bottom in the theatrical department (I did, in my early years) would make good practice for your goal. With practice, you'll learn that men are pretty much the same regardless of their exalted positions, and you will gain enormous self-confidence. David Stockman, who worked for a President, wrote "This always happened—every time I took a step up the ladder. You always thought that the people up on the next rung were going to be supermen. Few of them actually were.[1]" As you work your way up, you will find that men do not get more exciting or capable; their *positions* get more exciting. (No, not that kind of position. Their *jobs*.) Don't make rookie mistakes with your prime intended. Work out techniques on single men or on low-grade married men. Practice, practice, practice!

I suggest starting in high school. (But not, of course, with high school boys.) I waited until I was nineteen to start exploring my sexuality, and that left me with five years' worth of catching up to do. If you start early, some people may criticize you. If you are too open about your own personal goals, some people might try to interfere and steer you in other directions. If this happens, remember the good advice someone read to me: "Try to derive some comfort from the knowledge that if your guidance counselor were working up to *his* potential, he wouldn't still be in high school." Follow your own star. Or executive. Or author. Or politician.

As you practice, keep track of all the candidates that you consider. Remember the old saying that you should be nice to the people you meet on the way up, because you'll meet those people when you're going down. I suggest rating each prospect according to the criteria that are most important to you. The back of this book has an initial supply of the form that I use, but you can make your own. You will certainly include some of the criteria I mentioned, because they are proven. These prospect sheets will come in handy, because you'll find yourself back in Stage One after (or sometimes during) Stage Ten.

---

[1] I learned a lot, like this, from my mother. She's the one who's read the books and told me everything I know about things that happened before 1975 or so.

With these guidelines you can pick any man as your future beloved. Notice that I haven't said anything about your intended's wife. (I use "intended" because it's so much nicer than "target.") Sure, it helps if she is an independent career woman, ambitious, and not terribly attractive, with a few skeletons rattling around in her own closet. But you can pick your man regardless of his wife. If Hugh Grant can cruise curbside in Los Angeles while he has Elizabeth Hurley at home, think of the possibilities open to you!

You may wonder if your intended is really willing to have a relationship with you despite the solemn vows he once took. He is. Forget the Pope, but everyone else is on the "maybe" list. You shouldn't pick anyone dull (except for the occasional CFO, but that's just for practice), and as Erica Jong said, "Monogamy is impossible among interesting people." Married men usually feel guilty and want to stop the relationship, but they always come back. So follow my rules about picking your man, and then go for it!

"It's a great addition to my resume. It will be exciting. It's only for a short time, and it can't hurt."

—Monica Lewinsky

Stage 2
Getting Close

Having chosen your man, you must decide how to meet him. There are two ways: the **social route** and the **professional route**.

In the **social route**, you arrange to enter his social circle. There are many ways to do this.

The best way is to read about his activities. Remember, you've chosen a public figure, so he's in newspaper articles. The disadvantage of this approach is that it requires a lot of reading, and you must have better things to do than that. I suggest going through his trash instead. (Courts have ruled that trash placed on public streets is not constitutionally protected, so it's fair game. You won't want to go through the actual trash yourself, of course, but you should be able to get one of your male friends to do the dirty work at the cost of only one or two sweaty sessions on the couch. You don't even have to do anything that would cause you to brush your teeth or dry-clean your dress. Remember, men will do more in the *hope* of sex than they will for sex itself.)

You can learn where he plays golf, whether he likes horse races, what charities he supports, and so on. Then do what he does. Within limits, that is. Don't do anything that requires unflattering clothes or a lot of sweating while fully clothed. Charities are a particularly good way to meet your man, as long as you don't actually contribute to them. Instead of contributing, volunteer. Then you can appear at the charity's social functions. The better charities always have great dress-up functions. In fact, knowing the charities your man supports can help you decide if he really is a good candidate, based on whether he supports good charities or bad charities, how much he contributes, and how much he is out of the house.

Good charities include:

a. The Opera. No one attends opera unless they are rich or get tickets from their company, and you know that companies don't give tickets to people who are just "workers." So if your man attends the opera, you know that he has money, a good position, and time to waste—time that you could fill. You may have to actually go to an opera or two, though you should be able to avoid it. At worst, you might attend the opera but hang out in the bar while the awful music is going on. (If you do, first memorize the name of the opera, or even read the Classic Comics version of the story to prepare for intermission conversation.) That provides a good place for a "chance" encounter with your intended. Opera galas also let you wear your most fabulous dress, and off-the-shoulder items are not out of place, so you won't stand out when you move in for the kill. The perfect charity.

b. Public television. Similar to Opera in that it's only supported by people with too much money. Public television also has those dress-to-kill events. There's no danger of having to do real work as a volunteer, because what does your local public television station have to do besides raise money and write checks to buy programs from the BBC? If you're going to go all the way (more about that later!), you may have to watch a few PBS programs and then deny watching anything else on television. (If you do this be especially careful not to mention VH-1, and never mention MTV.) There's another benefit. After you start dating your catch, you can work the fund-raising telethons and wink to him whenever the camera shows the silent phone banks. The camera won't be on you very long, but it gives you chances for secret "hellos" during the five months out of the year that the station is doing its pledge drive.

c. Charities for fashionable diseases. Fashionable diseases are those that predominantly afflict minorities, women, and cute animals. AIDS, breast cancer, painful menopause, SAS (swollen ankle syndrome), harp seal cancer, bi-lingual dyslexia[2], tanning dysfunction, and so on. These organizations have their dressy events, and they are almost exclusively administrative. They move money and paper around, so there is little danger of you actually being next to people who have a disease. Those charities provide the added opportunity to meet leaders of the charity itself, who may be candidates for you. Such men may maintain a lower public profile than you like, but a life of limousines, charity-purchased townhouses, and first-class travel isn't all bad. (Before reading this guide, you would have scoffed at anyone dating the head of the National Baptist Convention or United Way! Be honest. You would have, wouldn't you?!)

It's even better if your man's charity is one of those organizations that raises money for other charities. They allow tons of

---

[2] Sufferers of this malady sometimes think the meaning of "is" is "yes."

"administrative expense" and run no risk of becoming involved with something as messy as curing a disease. Charities for the right diseases also give you an easy way to work into the conversation a tragic story about you or a dear friend or relative who had the disease and almost recovered, but not quite. The "you poor girl" reaction includes the innocent arm-around-the-shoulder, which accomplishes the all-important first touch and gives your man a free look down the front of your dress. (Don't worry if you don't have a tragic story. Tell one anyway. Your man isn't going to ask for proof. Just make sure that the tragic event occurred far away. You don't want your man to say "Why, I know the head of thoracic surgery at Mount Sinai. I'll talk to him about your twin sister's case." It's best to use one of the unknown South American locales from one of the frog-gives-birth-to-alien-genius (or vice versa) stories in the *Weekly World News*.)

Bad charities include:

a. The Rescue Mission. It's supported by guilty people, and you don't want a man who will feel guilty right from the start. Giving you gifts would then only make him feel *more* guilty. That's not the relationship you want! Also, the guilt of the supporters prevents them from going all out at their fund-raisers, and reduces the "fun quotient" to a really dreary level. You don't dress up in a ball gown, nibble caviar, and sip champagne while discussing plans to help the homeless. And rescue missions usually don't raise much money; they spend most of what they raise on the homeless; and they often expect you to get *involved*. As Tom Lehrer said, "Be careful not to do your good deeds when there's no one watching you."[3] Serving soup

---

[3] "Be Prepared"

with a huge spoon to someone who smells bad when there is no camera on you is *horrid*.

b. The Animal Shelter. While it may have some good affairs (as you plan to!), the people there expect volunteers to clean cages and to actually touch the animals. Ugh! You will have enough hurdles to overcome without trying to appear charming and desirable while you clean Fido-filth from under your fingernails.

c. Charities for unfashionable diseases. Unfashionable diseases are those that primarily affect men and ugly animals. Heart disease, prostate cancer, mole rat blindness, gout, executive stress, rat plague, and so on. You want to be associated with something you can talk about with friends, for goodness sake!

Charities are always good for fall-backs. If your man doesn't work out as a candidate (maybe because his wife is smart enough not to leave him alone at these affairs), charity balls are good places to prospect for better candidates. Why do you think they call them "balls"? Just as in real estate, the three keys are location, location, and location. You have to be in the right location to make the first contact.

If his trash doesn't show any sign of thank-yous from charities, look for a country club newsletter, flying magazines, health club notices, notices for upcoming meetings of Philanderers Anonymous, or other clues to locales where he might be found in a social setting. Then work your way into those settings. (What do you mean, "How?" There are *lots* of ways. Take golf or flying or fencing or tennis or whatever lessons to get near him. Visit the clubhouse at the golf course or the bar at the airport or the juice bar at the athletic club. Arrange a chance encounter and ask for help or advice or pointers.

Have you ever heard of a man *refusing* a chance to show an attractive, seductively dressed girl that he is smart or good at sports?)

Despite the many advantages of the social route, I recommend the **professional route**. That's the one that has worked best for me. In this route, you get a job where he works. You'll be spending a lot of money on clothes, cosmetics (especially lipstick), telephone bills, and, with luck, underwear, so it will help to get paid as you carry on your quest. You don't need to work *with* him or *near* him, just at the same location. There are always ways that you can meet, and I'll talk about those soon. First, I want to give you the only two criteria for a job near your candidate. It doesn't matter how much the job pays, or whether there is a chance for advancement (because that's not the route through which you'll advance), whether you will enjoy the work, whether you will be visible, or even if you'll have anything to do. But

The job has to let you move around the premises,

and

The job has to let you dress up.

You can't be chained to a desk[4], because you will have to move around to make contact. You may think that a visible position right up front would let you meet anyone you want, but beware. Never become a receptionist. You'll have to stay at one location and answer telephones. Yes, you will see your candidate and many other possible candidates. But you won't be able to initiate contact; you'll have to wait for them to come to you. And if you interrupt the conversation to answer the telephone, you give him a chance to move on. *Filling*

---

[4] Although that's an idea you may be able to use later when looking for ways to make your private time in his office more fun for both of you.

in for the receptionist for a week might be useful, because you can make the first contact there and then make your serious move later.

You have to dress up. Avoid jobs at places like loading docks (it's tough to work the loading dock in heels and a slit skirt and you often sweat a lot), cafeterias (the fishnet you want to wear doesn't go on your *head*), and supply rooms (where you might have to wear ugly, sensible shoes). You don't have to be outlandish, but you need to be able to wear dresses, hose, heels, and so on. I'll talk more about fashion at the next stage. For now, I'll just say that you need to pick a job that lets you look desirable. But as I learned when I studied psychology in college, every rule has an exception. If your man has particular tastes or fantasies, you could take a job that *doesn't* allow you to dress up but that *does* let you cater to those desires.

This is tricky, though. One common fantasy is of the sexy nurse. With some men, a nurse's uniform is enough to get them, shall we say, interested. (With *those* shoes? With *that* hose? Go figure. But it's true. Maybe it's the idea of sponge baths.) But it's hard to meet your man when dressed as a nurse, unless your choice is the 86-year-old-rich-man-with-a-bad-cough; that is, unless you're playing for keeps. That's not my style, so if that's your approach, I don't have much advice to offer. The most I can do is to offer to introduce you to Anna Nicole Smith. The other "fantasy" option is that of maid. I don't recommend that because you might have to *clean* something (other than his clock) and maids don't really get to wear those sexy French maid uniforms. Save the "dainty French maid bending over to dust the table" for one of your dates, in Stage Six.

Back to the professional route. Having gotten the job, you have to arrange to meet your candidate. The possibilities are limited only by your imagination. Here are a few that I recommend. How to flirt during these encounters is covered in Stages Four and Five.

1. The parking lot. Park in his reserved space, early enough before his usual arrival time that you can check your makeup. When he arrives, explain that this is your first day (this will work for the first few weeks) and that you'll be happy to move your car. (For this approach, make sure you dress or skirt will ride up to your belt when you get in your car to move it.)

2. The delivery. Arrange to deliver something to his office, even on the pretext of thanking him for the chance to work at such a wonderful company where the people are so friendly.

3. The lunch. Discreetly follow him to his favorite restaurant for lunch. (You won't be able to get much information from his secretary, because she knows what you're doing. She probably got her job by doing it with his predecessor. If she hasn't tried it with him herself, she will be protective of him. If she has tried it herself and failed, she will be bitter and out to screw you so you don't succeed where she failed.)

4. The happy hour. Again, you'll have to follow him. (Remember that discretion is still necessary. The flirting part comes later.) This is good because you'll find him relaxed and drinking. True, you'll follow him many times when he just goes home, but eventually you'll hit paydirt. So to speak.

5. The coincidence. Having gone through his trash, you can easily make up a reason to talk to him, because you know his hobbies and associations. Ploys like "My brother-in-law was in a failed land development deal, and the girls were talking about your land development, and I was wondering if I could have a few minutes of your time to ask how you avoided getting any blame for it?" or "My college room-mate turned $1000 into $100,000 in commodities, and I heard your wife was into commodities, so

I wondered if you could tell me how to avoid charges of insider trading?" or "My uncle just hired into a new company, and he fired the whole travel office so he could hire my cousins, and people here say you know all about travel, so could you tell me what reasons my uncle could give to pretend it wasn't just nepotism?" give your man a chance to show his brilliance. And to meet you. (But remember what I said earlier in this stage. Make sure all of the people you mention are in Puerto Mosquito da Luna, Chiletamale Province in a country you can't remember.)

6. Work. I left it until last, because it is the least desirable. But sometimes you may be forced to do some actual work, some work for him, that will bring you in contact. Avoid this if you can.

"I got everything ready. I put out what I was going to wear and had my hair cut."

—Monica Lewinsky

Stage 3
Planning the Encounter

You've chosen your man and have worked yourself into his presence. Eye contact has been established; your eagle has landed. You are anxious to start the fun part—the flirting—but don't do it yet. Your mother (or friends at the mall) told you not to be caught unprepared, and they were *soooo* right! You must be *ready* when he is available. There may not be time to run home for some quick cosmetic work. As the Boy Scouts say, be prepared. You must plan, plan, plan!

First, plan your wardrobe. You don't want to be caught after the first bout of subtle flirting wondering "What can I possibly wear next time?! Why do all my V-neck sweaters fit too loosely to show my bra straps?!" Make sure you have the dresses that open a little too much in front, the skirts that reveal the cute flesh just above the knee, the underwear that will be visible under your clothes, the quick-release buttons, and so on. Plan to accentuate your best features. (At a few isolated times in my life, I thought it was best to wear long dresses or slacks, to draw attention to my upper body and away from my lower. That brought my man's attention to my eyes and to other features that were of obvious interest to him. I used to wear a smart navy blue pantsuit, until it got stained, but I'll talk more about that in Stage Eight.) Remember, you only get one chance to make a first impression, so don't blow it.

A word to you girls who are—well, I guess I have to say it—flat-chested or nearly flat-chested. There are some men who like small-breasted women. I don't know any (well, I *wouldn't*, would I?), but I'm sure there are some. Even though it narrows the field of candidates, those are the men you under-endowed girls need to go after. *Do not wear artificial devices* ("Nature's Curves" or "Cleavage in a Box" or "Boobs-a-Lot" or whatever the info-mercials call them now). When the action with your man reaches the into-the-brassiere step, even optimists will see those cups as half-empty, not half-full. Unless you can do really, really amazing things with other parts of your body, the truth will be too much of a disappointment for your man, and you may lose him off your hook before he samples all of the bait. If you are mammary-challenged and still have your sights set on a man who likes breasts, you need to be able to answer "Yes" to two or more of these questions:

1. Can you juice oranges with your thighs?
2. Are any trailer hitches in your neighborhood now chrome-free?
3. Do you scratch the back of your neck with your ankle?
4. Can you eat an entire Popsicle without taking it out of your mouth (without your jaw hurting)?
5. Do you practice for dates by watching television with your knees and shoulders on the floor?
6. Do the English cucumbers in your refrigerator seldom make it into the salad?

7. Have you worn out more than one vibrator?
8. Does humming seem odd to you unless you have an ice cube and a banana in your mouth?

If you didn't pass this simple test, do yourself a favor and don't waste your time with bosom men. Don't fool yourself into thinking you can make up for your shortcoming in other ways. As a television character said many years ago, "Cup size trumps IQ."

Similarly, you girls who want to be blonde have to go totally blonde. "Hey, what's this?" is not the love talk you want to hear from your man (although the sound might be muffled when he says it). If you are not naturally blonde (and we know that only 16% of you are, dears) I advise against dyeing your hair. First, it raises the possibility that your man will find out before he is totally hooked on you. Second, I've found that dark hair blends better into the popular suit colors, anyway. (You will be dating someone who wears dark suits, if you follow the criteria in Stage One.) Wives can more easily spot the stray blonde hair on the dark suits your man wears.

Then, with the most important part of your life (the wardrobe) planned, get in shape! For you skinny little girls, put on some weight! I don't mean to carry this advice to the extreme that my former good friend Linda Tripp[5] did, but build some cushion! Sure, the men's magazines all show these cute hardbodies. But did you ever hear a man say "When she walked across the room, you should have seen her jugs stay motionless!"? You need some seductive sway, girls! You'd be amazed at what men notice. A successful businessman who can't see well enough to find his ball at the end of his putter (I'm talking golf here) will turn his head half-way around to watch

---

[5] I'm sorry, Linda dear. I won't say another word about you. Anyone who was portrayed by John Goodman on Saturday Night Live-and accurately portrayed, I might add-has suffered enough.

a sweater sway during warm-ups on the next fairway. And what do men talk about doing? Grabbing a piece of pelvic bone?

I recommend Ben and Jerry's ice cream. In fact, I recommend Ben and Jerry's ice cream for everything. It makes you feel better when you feel bad, it's a great treat when you feel good, it helps add those grab-able parts that men love so much. It's the best invention of the twentieth century. (Penicillin was good. It was *very* good, but that's another book.)

There is one essential supply that should always be in your purse. You can't be sure when you will be with your man, and you don't want things to get too messy. So follow the age-old advice, and keep this little packet in your purse at all times. It used to be the man's responsibility, but this is the age of women and equality, so we have to make the preparations. It's our responsibility, too. Yes, men usually have them, but your man may find it difficult to explain to his wife if she finds he has been buying them. It just takes up a little room in your purse, and it can save you so much. Yes, always keep that small pack of Kleenex.[6]

The other essential supply is a good lipstick. After my interview with dear Barbara Walters, sales of the lipstick I wore on that show soared. It's so important to have a good lipstick, and women knew that *my* lipstick had to be dependable. (You'll be going through *lots* of lipstick, and you don't want one that will go from you to him to the inside of his clothes.) Men love to see women wearing lipstick. (If you have any doubt, look at the female "news reporters" on television. If their purpose is to deliver serious news on Bosnia and the economy and advances in science, why do they all have bright red

---

[6] Kleenex is a registered trademark of Kimberly-Clark Corporation. They may not like being mentioned in this context (though how do they think they sell *box after box* of those things?), but I find that they really are the best. The triple-ply Cold Strength tissues can stand up to the most virile man when you're not.

lipstick? Because all the bleached-blonde women in television naturally put on lipstick when they get up at four o'clock in the morning? No. Because men like it. If men like it, do it.) Once you're successful with your man, you will be applying lipstick frequently, so buy the best you can afford.

Now that your wardrobe is ready, and your body is ready, and your purse is stocked, it's time to get him interested in you! On to Stage Four!

"I don't see sexuality as being something to hide away in the dark or be ashamed of."

—Monica Lewinsky

Stage 4
Subtle Flirting

Times have changed since my grandmother's day. Back in that century, women had to stand prettily, maybe expose an ankle, and hope that the man would send his servant to bring her to his estate. Or something like that. Since the fall of Communism, today's free-market economy is all about *competition*!

If you don't get your man, some little slut will. So you have to pursue him fiercely. (I might call the competition no-holds-barred, but I want to save that phrase for my advice about dating.) But always be ladylike. Men don't like sluts. (Well, actually they like sluts quite a lot. They like the way sluts dress—*du-uh*, that's why they dress that way—and the way they talk and the way they "date" and just about everything else about them. But they think that for sluts, the sex is enough, and so men don't have to give them any gifts. That isn't the full, meaningful relationship you want. You want sex *and* gifts. And the dignified self-respect that only an affair with a really prestigious married man can give you.) To be ladylike, your flirting must be *subtle*.

But your flirting must be subtle *as seen by the man*. This is entirely different from subtle as seen by a woman. A woman can see your eyes linger on a man for a fraction of a second longer than necessary and think "Why, that shameless hussy!" A man can have you lick peanut butter off his fingers during lunch and think "That poor girl must certainly have been hungry." You must be subtle and lady-like, but still penetrate his consciousness.

By now, everyone knows about hitching up your jacket to give him a peak at your thong underwear as a way of showing that you find him charming, intelligent, and a possible soul-mate. That's a dandy opening gambit; it's good enough that it may enable you to skip a lot of other gambits. But there are other ladylike, subtle ways to get your man's attention. When he's looking at you, lick your lips. Not in an offensive way, of course. Just enough to say "Boy, are my lips dry. I don't how I can keep them wet!" Make subtle references to movies that made you horny. (If you pick foreign films, this also lets him see your cultural side.) Mention your dreams of a meaningful relationship with a sensitive, caring man (what man would *not* pretend to be sensitive and caring if he thought it might get him into an alluring set of pants?). Giggle if he ever mentions the words *moon*, *frigate*, or *lay* (even as part of "Frito-Lay"), or says he used a restaurant's rear entry.

There are countless opportunities to flirt. You will have prepared your wardrobe, including the all-important V-neck sweater. When wearing it, arrange to hand something to your man. (In Stage Two I suggested meeting him by delivering things to his office. Delivering a pizza is always fun, since it also gives you chances to lick your lips.) When you do, remember elbows *in*. That should give you plenty of cleavage right in his natural line of sight, and he'll surely notice what you'd *like* to give him.

Casual remarks that can be taken two ways are fun for you and for him. Innocent remarks like "These bras with the clasp in the front are *so* much easier than the old-fashioned kind" may just get him to notice you in other than a professional way. And if he's a little slow on the uptake, as so many men are, when he looks directly at your chest you can say "With the old kind I used to have to reach waaay back here" as you put both of your hands behind your back. (Remember to throw your shoulders back. He'll notice more, and there will be more to notice.) I've had success with clever, subtle, double-entendre remarks like "Gosh, I wish I had something that would reach the tickle that's *way* in the back of my throat." Remarks like that also show him that you are intelligent and have a good sense of humor, because they can mean so many things.

Arrange to get next to him, but overshoot the mark so your prime parts bump into him. (This is another reason you want "soft," girls.) You don't even have to excuse yourself. He will pretend not to notice, and he might even think it is accidental. You may have to bump other parts before he begins to catch on that you are not clumsy. If he doesn't seem to be a "front" man, there are always subtle ways to back into him. If he stands behind his desk and reaches for something, say "Let me get that for you!" then squeeze between him and his desk and bend way over to get what he wants. If he thinks this is an accident, repeat it. (Like the directions say, get him in a lather once, then repeat.)

No matter what else you do, always at some point bring up the subject of those poor men whose wives don't understand them, and make it clear that you sympathize with the men. You can start innocently, by saying how you hope someday to be married and be the ideal wife, not like those hard, shrewish wives who don't understand how hard their husbands work and the fact that their husbands have needs and that of course a man is always going to look at pretty girls but it doesn't mean that he doesn't love his wife and that the really important thing is that a man providing for his wife is the real way he shows he loves her without roses and jewelry and mushy cards on "holidays" that Hallmark made up and that you hope you won't be a wife like that. That is absolutely guaranteed to get him to start looking at you as a real possibility. All men (at least all successful men) think that their wives don't appreciate all the work they do to provide a good living, and all men will look at pretty women even if they are completely in love with their wives. (Charlie Chaplin said "Every man, whether he be young or old, when meeting any woman, measures the potentiality of sex between them." And Charlie Chaplin did a lot of measuring.) Showing that you understand gives him a chance to bring out the my-wife-doesn't-understand-me routine that he's going to get to sooner or later anyway. And it lets him blame his wife for the hot monkey sex he's going to have with you. So you have to bring this up. If you do, it won't be the only thing you bring up, I promise. (But after you are successful, remember to bring this up again. *Wives* should understand that their husbands love them because they pay the rent and spend holidays with them and put food on the table. But since he doesn't do those things for you, *you* could use a little token to show that he loves you for more than just sex. Since he probably *does* love you only for sex, he will go overboard to try to show that he *doesn't*. That can mean some nice little gifts for you.)

As the police in crime novels say, all of this should give him the opportunity and the motive. He already has the weapon. But some men are slow. If yours doesn't take the bait, even when you dangle it in front of him, it's time to move to Stage Five.

"He had this big 50th birthday party...he was talking to a whole bunch of people in and around my area and I had...my back to him and I kind of put—put my hand behind me and touched him [in the crotch area]."

—**Monica Lewinsky**

Stage 5
Advanced Flirting

If your subtle flirting hasn't worked, it's time to move on to advanced flirting. Your man is obviously the kind who doesn't pick up subtle hints. So if you've picked an insurance company executive, gynecologist, high-level government official, movie star, or someone similarly lacking in sensitivity, it's time to be just a little less ladylike and a little more determined.

One way is to use comments that, unlike the clever and ambiguous remarks in Stage Four, have a direct sexual meaning. Ideally, you will show that you are intelligent as well as available. Discussing politics is a good way to do this. There is always some way to bring up Justice Clarence Thomas. Almost every conversation has something vaguely related to the law, or to women, or to men, or to jobs, or to Congress. And men love to feel that they are getting an unfair deal. Casually say "I don't know what the big deal with Clarence Thomas was about. So what if he put a pubic hair on a can of Diet Coke? I've *spit up* pubic hairs while drinking Diet Coke." It's a good bet that your man will respond with a remark that isn't about Diet Coke.

Another advanced flirting technique involves surprising your man. Sneak into his office and hide under his desk. When he sits down and finds you there, explain that you were looking for your morning protein drink. It should not take too many references like this before he starts to catch on.

Follow up on the "subtle flirting" techniques. In subtle flirting, you wear a V-neck sweater. In advanced flirting, you drop a paper clip down it and ask for help. In subtle flirting, you lift up a piece of clothing to display your thong underwear. In advanced flirting, you lift up a piece of clothing to show your thong underwear, but forget to wear it. In subtle flirting, you casually brush up against him. In advanced flirting, you do the same thing, but you tend to stick.

You have to do it a little differently in public, such as at a public event or at a meeting. I would position myself in front of my man, and when I turned around to walk away, I'd gently and surreptitiously caress his crotch. That may sound brazen, but remember that if subtle flirting had worked for you, you wouldn't have had to go through this stage. If you want to remain demure, you can cover it up with a quick remark like "Oh. I'm sorry! I meant to wave, but you were just *there*!" Eroticism *plus* a compliment on his size. What man could resist?

Men are visual creatures. While we women are excited only by romantic thoughts and atmosphere and loving, caring men, men can be turned on just by seeing an attractive woman. In fact, men can be turned on by seeing attractive *parts* of *unattractive* women. It's difficult for women to understand this. To see what it's like, wait until the end of a long, hard day and then stare at a large bowl of Ben and Jerry's New York Super Fudge Chunk just outside your reach. It will immediately provoke the "lick" response. That's what it's like being a man, except that instead of cool, soothing, satisfying ice cream, the mere thought of "thigh" can provoke the response. (Some men even get aroused when reading the menu at KFC.) So take advantage of this. If your man is really hard to get, I have two words for you: Sharon Stone. Or four words: Sharon Stone, *Basic Instinct*. Practice crossing your legs. In "subtle" flirting, you cross your legs to expose a lot of thigh. In advanced flirting, you cross your legs *flamboyantly*. Let's just say that a good bikini wax is really important for this.

You can give him little gifts that show that you care about him in more than a professional way. Here are some ideas:

1. An anatomically correct paperweight always reminds him that you could be in front of him any time he chooses.

2. A cake in a shape with a special meaning to him shows that you are sensitive to his wants. I once gave a birthday cake in the shape of a favorite lizard to a man I was using for practice, and the cake turned out not to be the dessert, if you know what I mean.

3. A favorite book of limericks can express your deep emotion, especially if you bookmark and underline selected short ones so he doesn't actually have to read the book.

4. A pair of coffee *mugs* from Starbucks would be useful and for me it has led to one of those clever word-plays that highlights your intelligence and one of your best assets.

5. A cellular telephone with your number on speed-dial and a note saying that he can press your button anytime.

Another advanced flirting technique is to lay your feelings wide open for him, suggesting that that's not all you'd lay wide open for him. I told one man (who shall remain nameless, as he will throughout this entire book) "I have a really big crush on you." That seemed to get through to him. When all else fails, be bold.

"The emotional and friendship aspects...developed after the beginning of our sexual relationship."

—Monica Lewinsky

Stage 6
Dating

You made it! Your man has taken the hints and you've connected. Now for the fun part: Dating! Even "rug dates" can be special (see below).

Of course, since your man is married, you won't be taking carriage rides through Central Park together (unless it's in your Halloween costumes). You will have a limited number of places in which you can meet, so be flexible, both psychologically and physically. Expect to meet in secret, special places (often his office), where the thrill of possible discovery adds to the excitement. Try storage rooms, meeting rooms, closets, and bathrooms[7], as well as his office. Variety adds spice, and spice is nice!

In some rare cases, you might have to bring your man along slowly. If he feels he needs to "get to know you" or "trust you" first, he may only go to third base with you and not let you get that RBI. If that happens, make sure that a sink or flowerpot is nearby to serve as home plate. (An occasional squirt of protein might even help the plant

---

[7] What a bathroom lacks in soft furniture it makes up for with a lockable door, towels, and lotions.

grow!) Or you can use your Cold Strength Kleenex. (You *have* been paying attention, haven't you?)

Remember the normal sequence of attachment in affairs of the heart. First comes a *physical* relationship. Then comes a *sexual* relationship. Then comes an *emotional* relationship. So don't be surprised if your man trusts you enough to put his family jewels in your mouth, but needs that last step of an emotional relationship before he can let you give them that final buffing.

The fact that the time and location of your soul-bonding encounters will be limited does not mean your dates have to be boring. A little imagination can lead to lots of different kinds of dates. Some of my favorites:

1. The Desk Date. On this date, you and your man make your special kind of love on or under his desk.

2. The Rug Date. On this date, you and your man make your special kind of love on his rug.

3. The Sofa Date. On this date, you and your man make your special kind of love on his sofa.

4. The Wall Date. On this date, you and your man make your special kind of love while one of you leans against a wall.[8]

5. The Ottoman Date. On this date, you and your man make your special kind of love on his ottoman.[9]

6. The Sofa and Ottoman Date. You're going to have to figure this one out for yourself. Sometimes it hurts.

---

[8] The choice of direction is up to you.

[9] I recommend this only if your special kind of love involves one of you bending backward or forward.

A special word of advice: You have to be especially good at something. (Remember my advice to practice, practice, practice!) You have to outshine the other girls he's had and can have. You have to outshine his wife, too, but that's easy. They do the same thing every time, they don't do it often enough because there are always household concerns, they never do it in unusual places because the kids are always around, he falls asleep immediately after they do it, she's often not in the mood after a full day of taking care of the house (or hiring household help), he can never suggest anything exotic because if she disapproves she'll never let him forget how perverted he is and she'll always wonder where he learned of it, and they've generally fallen into a routine. The best advice was given by an ancient Greek[10]. He said "The fox knows many tricks. The hedgehog only one. One *good* one." Whether your specialty is oral pleasure, using sex toys, phone sex, toe-sucking, straightforward penetration, non-straightforward penetration (don't even *ask!*), or something else, be the *best* at it.

Be the best at one thing, but don't let that be the *only* thing you do. As I said, variety is the spice of life. Try different positions. Perfume different parts of your body. Couple in different ways. Bring mink-lined handcuffs. Use Altoids. Don't let any possibility escape your notice. Let your imagination run free. Get him to suggest his fantasies. If he secretly desires to be whipped with wet fettucine while his thighs are wrapped with duct tape and he makes love to a casaba melon, do it! Remember that unlike his wife *you* will never say "Why you perverted, disgusting piece of filth!" Remember what a respected television news anchorman once said: "An ounce of perversion is worth a pound of cure." And your man will love you for it.

---

[10] By the way, don't rule out "Greek" as a possible specialty.

Now that the sex part has been established and you have gratified him (or each other, if you're lucky), it's time to start talking. You want to make sure that you have connected with your sexual soulmate. Talk, talk, talk! Start by making sure that he knows your name. One neat trick is to wear a headband with your name on it.[11] Once you're confident that he knows your name, you can move on to *feelings*. You'll talk about your emotional connection, about how you admire him, about being playful, about your possible future together, about the relationship being based on more than just sex. At that last part, he'll probably suddenly kiss you and shove your hand down his pants, as his way of changing the subject. Once you're finished with *that* business, you can go back to talking.

See if you can get him to declare his need for you, even his dependence on you. He may even say that the fifteen minutes you spend together is the best part of his day. Try to believe this, because it will make you feel so much better about yourself. See if he asks questions about *your* dreams and hopes and cute little thoughts. Make sure he wants to know you for *yourself*, not just for your breasts or hands or special abilities. A true love connection is the best way to ensure that the relationship lasts, off and on, for several years. (See Stage Seven.) Or at least until you've gotten what you need. (See Stage Eight, and, eventually, Stage Ten.)

Since everybody has heard about this anyway, I might as well tell you about it. Everyone knows my favorite method of getting around problems like my man being busy, or spending time with his family, or being tied up at the office.[12] Phone sex. Everyone talks about it (now), but apparently many people don't understand it. When Barbara Walters asked me how it worked, she asked the question as

---

[11] But be sure that the name faces up, so he can read it as he looks down at the top of your head. And beware if he starts calling you "Nike." That spells "cheating on you."

[12] I *told* you to be open to everything.

if she didn't know the answer. (Now that I think about it, I can believe that she really doesn't.) So here's a step-by-step explanation, but pardon me if I have to get a little graphic. (I'll leave out the really graphic (that is, effective) parts, but this is still *soooo* embarrassing!)

1. Pick a time when your man will be physically alone. He can be at work or at home or on the road, as long as no one can actually see him at the moment.

2. Wear a loose-fitting garment, or maybe no garment at all. Get comfortable on a sofa, your bed, or an upholstered chair. (Pressing backwards into a cane-backed chair can leave marks on your back that take three days to go away. Then it would be no strapless dresses during *those* days!)

3. After the usual brief chatter about the deep emotional attachment you share, start talking about how you miss him. Then about what parts of him you miss. Then what you would like to do to those parts. Then what you would like him to do to *your* parts.

4. Be graphic. It may be difficult at first, but that's one reason you practiced with those other men. Be completely open about your body, his body, and how various parts of them fit together. Men love women who are forthright in that way. (But instead of "forthright in that way" they call it "talking dirty.") Don't talk about "enveloping him in a warm, passionate embrace." Talk about "smothering him with your breasts, feeling his hot tongue tasting your straining nipple." Don't talk about him possessing you. Talk about his hand reaching inside you, filling your emptiness and being drenched in the flow of your love juices as he drives you wild, wild with his hands over every part of your hot, steaming love canal.

5. Oh, God! Where was I?

6. As you both talk about what you would do if you could reach each other with your hands and mouths and body parts and chocolate sauce and pillows and bananas and

7. Where was I, again?

8. Oh, yes. As you discuss exactly (and I mean exactly) what you would like to do, you each take matters into your own hands at each end of the phone. With phone sex, you let your fingers do the walking. Keep going until your words are interrupted by your moans, and you finally climax with a release of incredible energy, draining him and invigorating you, and the warm afterglow suffuses your entire body and he starts to get sleepy.

One way he can show that he truly cares for you is to have *him* call *you* for phone sex. With your cell phone, he can call you anytime. If you live with your mother and have confided in her, she won't mind you excusing yourself to take the call in another room.[13] If you're at a restaurant, you can excuse yourself to the ladies room and complete the entire thrilling call there (though that is why I'm no longer welcome at Spago's). If you've just stepped out of the shower, you can pretend that you are lounging in sexy lingerie flipping through the *Rubiyat* of Omar Khayyam and nibbling dates. (That's "dates" as in the fruit.) That's one of the best things about phone sex. You don't have to do your hair, you don't have to do your nails, you don't have to squeeze into that dress he likes that doesn't fit anymore. In fact, if he's in the mood and you're not (that happens), you can even read or sort clothes while you're doing it. Men are so *easy* to fool.

---

[13] But in this case, keep the moaning down. Mothers *know* what their daughters do, but they still don't want to *hear* it.

I like to keep records of my dating. They can be so handy for your blow-by-blow descriptions to your intimate, trustworthy circle of a dozen or so friends. They are also useful memory-joggers whether you eventually take Route Paula Jones or Route Gennifer Flowers in Stage 10, or if you need to establish your credibility in some messy independent quasi-legal witchhunt. I keep track of when, where, what, how, and how many times, as well as some key likes and dislikes of the man I'm dating, using the Contact Record form that I've included at the back of this book. You can tear it out to use as-is, or make your own custom form, depending on what you want to record.

An essential part of the dating stage is *getting* gifts. That's part of what keeps the relationship strong on your part, so I talk about that in the next stage.

"The reason why those phone conversations were so important to the relationship was because they were safe—neither one of us worried that someone would walk in."

—Monica Lewinsky

Stage 7

Keeping the Relationship Strong

You've won your man and are having a lot of fun on your "dates." But you can't relax. Remember, dating is a competitive sport and free agency is rampant. There are always women younger than you, a few prettier than you, some more ambitious than you. Your main advantage is that there are none more *dedicated* or *prepared* than you. You need to devote the time and attention it takes to keep your relationship strong. As usual, there are a few main ways of accomplishing this.

A quick explanation: In this book I give only a few simple rules for each stage. That's because when dealing with men, there are always only a few things to remember. The reason is that men are so *simple*. They want the respect of other men, the admiration of women (mostly expressed through sex), and, occasionally, a good cheeseburger. Everything else doesn't matter very much. They work hard at their jobs so they can make money and get women. They buy fancy cars so their buddies will look up to them and so they can get women.

They buy nice clothes so they can get women. They go into politics so they can get elected to office, get the respect of other men, and get *lots* of women. Men are so simple that they usually talk about *facts* rather than *feelings*, they think that *they* seduce *women* instead of what really happens, and they get excited about a game with nine men standing around waiting for something to happen. How much do you have to know to deal with them? So I offer only four rules for keeping the relationship strong.

Give the right gifts. Give him gifts that make him remember you. Hickeys are fun, but they are not advised, especially if your man is photographed a lot. I suggest a box of cigars. The kind of cigar depends on the stage of your relationship.

If you two are still in the "tentative" stage of dating, doing no more than meeting for hot bouts of fondling and oral sex, I suggest a box of Lonsdales (usually about a 42 ring gauge). If you have moved on to the "serious" stage, with full intercourse in private and those oh-so-delicious semi-public places, go for the Robustos. They are more filling, but still not large enough for the deepest relationship. If you are lucky enough to reach the "soul-mate" stage, in which you share your deepest thoughts and emotions for up to five minutes at a time (but to consider yourself in this stage *both* of you have to talk!), then it's time for a box of Churchills. Another advantage of cigars is that they go up in smoke, so his wife won't be asking him "Where did that gold-tipped unicorn statue on your night stand come from?"

A clever trick is to give him something that he will use every day, because that will remind him of you. If he uses cigars for smoking, you can give him a cigar lighter. A cigar lighter is like a cigarette lighter, except that it has a flame that is as tall and straight as—well, it's tall and straight. This is small enough for him to keep in his pocket or at the office, and won't raise questions from his wife. If he wants to brag, he can bring it out in front of his male friends and tell stories about wonderful you who gave him the lighter, as well as so many happy minutes. But the best gift is *ties*.

At first you might think "Lots of people give him ties. I want to stand out." But that's just the point. You have to give him something his wife won't question. He can always tell her he forgets who gave him the red tie with green frogs, but he isn't very likely to get away with that if she sees him putting on boxer shorts with "WIDE LOAD" written across the front. Ties have so many advantages.

1. As I said, the wife isn't likely to question a tie.

2. You can give ties as many times as you wish, while once you give your man the "Hole-Me-In-One" office putting set, he's pretty well set for grassy holes.

3. He can send you secret signals by wearing one of your ties in public or on important days at the office.

4. You can *personalize* a tie for him. You can't write your name on it, but you can give it your own special scent. And I don't mean perfume.

5. You can sneak a tie into his office under your dress.

Of course, you will expect him to reciprocate with little symbols of his true love and caring for you. Sweaters, little diamond trinkets, books, and so on. Encourage him in this, but stress that the gifts are just reminders of him when you can't be together. You may try the beggar's line from *Kismet*: "I don't need any luxuries. Just lots of necessities will do." Keep all of his gifts, even if some of them are typical "man" gifts like power appliances or ugly jewelry or how-to books or picture books about the 1955 Chevrolet. They will all remind you of him, and they may be useful in one of the later, less enjoyable stages of your relationship. But most of all *get those gifts*.

Here is another little trick I use. I keep track of all the gifts I give and all the gifts I get. I want to be sure that I know when my man is wearing one of my ties, or quoting from one of my books, or using one of my cigars. And of course I record all the gifts he gives me. This helps me keep track of the progress of the relationship. A decline in the quality of his gifts is a sure sign that he's starting to take you for granted, and you may have to show him another side of you to keep him interested. (There are some things you can do when you run out of sides, but those aren't for beginners.) At the back of this book, I've included some of the Gift Register forms I use. These records also come in handy as a checklist if you need to deposit his gifts with a friend for safe-keeping before a subpoena is served.

Compliment him. You know what compliments to give. No matter what your man's main member is like, tell him how large he is. Every man will eat that up. (Wait, that's your job. *Ooooh*, another double-entendre. See how easy it is?) This doesn't mean that you have to lie. Just think of him as the olive in your martini of life. Have you ever looked at cans of olives in the supermarket? The *smallest* grade you can buy is "large." If your man is even *close* to average, he's "*sooo large!*" If he's average, use a more superlative adjective.[14]

Of *course* he'll believe it. Which one do you think a man would believe: the objective evidence of a ruler, or a fawning girl moaning in ecstasy at his jumbo colossal equipment? If you even have to *think* about that question, go back and re-read about men in the first part

---

[14] For reference, here are the official USDA grades for olive sizes: large, extra large, mammoth, giant, jumbo colossal, and super colossal. I won't go into how you can grade your man, but here's where your practice comes in handy. Remember, the smallest man you ever know is at least *large*.

of this stage. We girls know the truth in that old song "It Ain't the Meat, It's the Motion," but no matter how confident a man is, he secretly believes that the motion just isn't enough. That's one reason that many men don't practice at being better lovers. They believe in the saying "Quality can be replaced by quantity and morale." They are so endearing when they *try* so hard without having any idea of what they're doing. So you have to build him up, even if you sometimes need to stifle an inappropriate yawn.

Some readers may think I'm focusing too much on sex. They will ask "Why do you only talk about *that kind* of compliment? What about complimenting his clothes, his hair, the masterful way he runs his job?" Sure, you should compliment him on those things. I've found that it helps to refer to him by pet names like "Handsome." But which of these do you think a man would most like to hear:

1. "It's so amazing how you got the Arabs and Israelis to disarm and swear to live in harmony forever!"

2. "Einstein would be so astounded at your discovery of the unified field theory explaining all the forces in the entire universe, after he failed for decades to find it!"

3. "Why, your genetic engineering of the super-potato could end world hunger, purge the environment of harmful chemicals, and restore the ozone layer!"

4. "Congratulations for inventing the Internet!"

5. "No man has *ever* had a tool that could fill me up *half* as much as you do!"

Of course.

Make it easy for him. Of course, *you* are "easy" for him. But make the whole relationship easy for him. Go to *his* office. Telephone him when *he* has free time (and Kleenex). Don't ask for large gifts that his wife will see him sneaking out of the house with. Don't insist that he do things that he doesn't want to do. Someone said "The problem with having a mistress is not the screwing part, it's having to eat dinner twice in one night." You don't want him to see you as a burden. You have limited time together; you knew he was a busy man when you started this. So conform to his schedule. If he has to make an important phone call while he's making you, keep your voice down. (Unless he's talking to a priest, background cries of "Oh, God!!" will be difficult for him to explain.) If you are servicing him orally while he's conducting business on the phone, time his climax so it happens when the *other* person is speaking, so your man's voice doesn't change at a bad moment. (I suppose it's possible that he could normally close business deals with heartfelt cries of "Yes!! Yes!! Now!! Now!! You're so good!!" But it isn't likely.)

And most important, **keep him satisfied just enough.** As the saying goes, "If you get them by the balls, the hearts and minds will follow." The saying is true, and you are going to use particularly pleasurable equipment to do it. As I've said before, you want to do things for him that his wife doesn't do[15], you want to be available to him, you never want to have a headache, you want to shine in at least one sexual act, you want to practice variety, and you generally want to be his ideal fantasy woman. Almost.

You should not be available *every* time he wants you. Eighty percent, ninety percent, of the time, maybe. But not 100%. I studied psychology in college. I learned that a rat will press a lever more industriously if the rewards are sporadic than if he never gets a

---

[15] This is the easiest part. Even the two words "You're good" will usually accomplish this.

reward or always gets a reward. Also in college I learned that men are pretty much like rats. The *promise* of sex is more powerful than sex itself. That's why you keep flirting even after you've hooked him, because the flirting promises sex that he won't have right now. If a pie is just out of reach, a man will drool; if he can bury his face in the pie, he's satisfied after a few minutes. (Maybe I should have picked another analogy, but you get the idea.)

*"I don't clean all my clothes right after I wear them.
I usually don't clean them again until I know I'm
going to wear them again."*

—Monica Lewinsky

Stage 8
Boasting and Gathering Evidence

Let's remind ourselves of the reason you're in this temporarily wonderful relationship. You are looking for love and self-respect, with a few semi-precious mementos thrown in. How are you going to get that self-respect? By talking to your friends about the really important man who loves you sporadically.

Maybe I shouldn't have called this "boasting." It's simple girl-talk, sharing feelings, emotions, what's going on in our lives. It just helps if what's going on in your life is "Dean Bugger had me over for the weekend. No, I mean he *had* me over for a *whole* weekend." If what's going on in your life is "My cat Priscilla Queen of the Desert coughed up another fur-ball all over my dry-cleaning," the conversation will tend to center around the other people in the group. You need to have the good stories, the impressive accomplishments, the important connections, the inside scoops, the delicious tidbits. You need to tell your friends about your *man*. But to avoid coming off as boastful, make sure you disguise this as a search for support. You can say "He canceled a meeting with the Japanese Ambassador so he could lick lint out of my navel and he said I was the most important thing in the world to him and that he has never felt like this about anyone ever before, but he can't see me next Tuesday at 8:00." Or "We made love for six hours straight and he was so handsome and he brought me the most gorgeous opal necklace from Harrod's where he ditched his wife in the French Cheese section so he could shop for me but he forgot my name again."

I recommend telling at least ten or eleven friends about your relationship That should be enough to spread your fame throughout your social circle. And, their recollections (and if you're lucky, tape recordings) can be useful in the last and saddest stage of your relationship. Whether you tell your mom is a delicate decision. (You *never* tell your father, because he thinks that no man is good enough for his daughter. Especially a man whom she visits in secret for up to half an hour at a time.) If your mom is a rock of solid support through all manner of sordid dealings, if she has properly indulged you throughout your life, if the concept of discipline has not been an integral part of your relationship, if she has given you pointers on quick-release undergarments, if you expect to need her as a corroborating witness, then by all means tell her.

No relationship lasts forever. (Well, I've read of some really old people who have been married for a long, long, time—but those are old people, not young people like us.) You need to protect yourself just in case. "Covering your ass" can have more than one meaning and you never know when reality will come crashing in and people will start taking just everything out of context. So here are my tips for, shall we say, *documenting* what really happened.

1. Remind your friends of your side of the story. Keep their memories fresh.

2. Save telephone answering machine tapes. Especially of the phone sex. Especially when *he* called *you*. Not only will they show the mutual aspect of the relationship, but you may want to play back a few of them on evenings when Blockbuster is out of *Casablanca*.

3. Don't delete those e-mails. Computer people can find the date that each one was created, so they can serve as a historical record of what you felt when. (I mean, a record of what you were feeling. I mean, a record of what was going on inside you. Oh, never mind. Just keep them.)

4. Record any distinguishing physical characteristics your man has. If you can describe the angle of the dangle or the lane of the vein or the curve of the cue-stick, it will be hard for anyone to deny the intimate bond that you shared.

5. Keep the gifts, the signed photographs, the news photos showing your important man with you always hovering nearby.

6. Remember the old adage "Dry-clean in haste, repent at leisure." Sometimes the perfect piece of physical evidence will fall right into your lap. Or onto your blouse. Or onto the special panty-hose with the extra opening. If it happens, keep that clothing. If your wardrobe is limited, you may need to clean that item just before you wear it again, but try to put it away as a loving memento and as incontrovertible biological evidence. If you need to prove your relationship, bring out the clothing and have it DNA-tested. Even *sperm* can't wiggle out of that one.

7. Until useful body fluids come your way, keep some un-smudged fingerprints from one of the gifts he's given you, or from a little item you lift from his office.

"I was hysterical all weekend. All I did was cry and eat pizzas and sweets."

—Monica Lewinsky

Stage 9
Getting Dumped

Your relationship can't last forever. When it starts to unravel, handle it gracefully. It's your turn to be the adult. You will go through the phases of dumping, just like the stages of death, including denial ("He can't be getting tired of me. He must have just been too tired or busy to see me."), anger ("And after I wore my knees to the bone for him!"), bargaining ("What if I learn to hold *two* ice cubes in my mouth?"), and acceptance ("I never really loved him anyway.") Dumping has an extra phase at the beginning, and it's the only phase that's enjoyable: the binge phase.

In the binge weekend, dietary rules are suspended, calories are nullified, and you eat everything you ever wanted. All in one weekend. Food, you can always depend on. So confirm the fact that your life does have one permanent, unchanging, bedrock. Double-cheese pizza, See's candy, Godiva truffles, Ben and Jerry's ice cream, potato chips, caramel sauce straight from the bottle, pie topped with whipped cream, whipped cream topped with whipped cream, jelly beans, Oreos, double-stuffed Oreos, cake, cake topped with whipped cream, cake topped with Oreos, moo goo gai pan, moo goo gai pan half an hour later (but the fortune cookie will make you cry!), pepperoni pizza with extra sausage, sausage pizza with extra pepperoni, calzones, calzones with extra sausage. All the food that really loves you. The food that loves you so much it wants to stay with you forever. Unlike *him*.

After the binge weekend, you will start to realize that you didn't really love him, that he was a big jerk more of the time than he was your real soul-mate, that his musings about "Who knows what will happen four years from now?" didn't mean "Maybe I'll be divorced and we can get married and do those fun, couple-y things," but "Who knows where *you* will be four years from now?"

The breakup can be painful. The only preventative step you can take is to make sure you are the dumper and not the dumpee. If you find that he is drifting away from you, first try to win him back; if you think that the breakup will be permanent, win him back and then you dump him. You have to be attuned to the signals. Look for these telltale signs that his attention is wandering:

1. He starts forgetting your name again and resorts to "Kiddo."

2. For your playful experiments with cigars, he switches from hand-rolled to machine-made.

3. He starts forgetting to say hello before unhooking your bra.

4. He stops suggesting that he may be divorced in a few years.

5. You find someone else's kneepads under his desk.

6. His secretary starts smiling instead of frowning when you visit his office.

7. He falls asleep during your soulful conversations.

8. During your dates, naked time exceeds clothed time.

You might use some subtle encouragement to get him to keep seeing you. One way is to hint at revealing your relationship. (Remember one of the reasons in Stage One that you picked a public figure?) During one of your dates, you could casually mention that you've toyed with the idea of writing an autobiography. Be careful how you word this. Saying something like "I'm thinking about exposing you" may get him excited instead of worried. You don't want this to be a *threat*, because men react against threats (threats challenge their manhood). It's more along the lines of "Gosh, we have such a good relationship and you've told me I'm so important to you that I think we should share with other people the wonderful companionship and support we've found in each other. Do you happen to know the phone number of the Washington *Post*?" (Substitute "New York *Times*" or "Chicago *Tribune*" or "Atlanta *Journal-Constitution*" or whatever newspaper is appropriate. "Appropriate" doesn't mean "the one with the widest circulation." It means "whatever newspaper his wife is most likely to read.") If this doesn't get his attention, start carrying a copy of *The Star* or another tabloid around with you and idly speculating on how much money they pay for stories. If he doesn't notice, perhaps a more sensitive friend of his will notice and explain his risk to him.

Your self-esteem will suffer. This will be a difficult time. But you already know the two rules that apply in this case. First, get even. (That's Stage Ten.) Second, when you get tossed off a stallion, you have to climb right back on top. (Or underneath. Whatever.) In your case, it will be a different stallion, and you'll go back to Stage One.

"And she [Linda Tripp] said 'Monica, promise me you won't sign the affidavit until you get the job. Tell Vernon you won't sign the affidavit until you get the job, because if you sign the affidavit before you get the job, they're never going to give you the job.'"

—**Monica Lewinsky**

Stage 10
Getting Even

Your self-respect has suffered a serious blow. You no longer have the best stories in your circle of girlfriends. You gained 15 pounds during your binge weekend and some of your favorite clothes don't fit anymore. Someone must pay.

First, collect your evidence. The e-mails, the circled dates on your calendar, the lovingly preserved stains. Then decide on your route to justice.

You can take one or both of two routes. You can get paid off, or you can cash in directly.

The **payoff route** (I call it Route Paula Jones) can take one of two forms. You can get a cash settlement in partial compensation for your heartbreak and for the shattering of the hopes and dreams you had when you first insinuated yourself into the presence of this married public figure and flirted him into your pants. If this is your prefer-ence, I strongly urge you to reach a private settlement. Just as a few flashes of your thong were enough to start the whole relationship, a few flashes of autographed gifts, a few snippets of "Hi. What are you wearing?" telephone tapes, a few e-mails from friends asking you to confirm some of his more unusual sexual practices should be enough to make him realize that he should do his best to make you whole, only with his checkbook this time. If they aren't, you may have to take the legal avenue. The legal avenue is fraught, indeed veritably fraught, with pitfalls. These include:

1. There are opposing lawyers, which will make the whole thing ugly. Since they are lawyers, you cannot expect them to have any regard for modesty, truth, fairness, restraint, or ethics. (If the "Legal Ethics" course in law school is really about ethical lawyers, it's an *archeology* course.)

2. Lawyers will bring out your whole sexual history. It doesn't matter what's admissible in court. What matters is what's admissible in the media. If the media runs reports of cigars in vaginas, ejaculation into sinks, conducting business during oral sex, preferences about breast size, distinguishing physical characteristics, semen, whether sex is defined as *his* mouth on *her* genitals or only *her* mouth on *his* genitals, and what the meaning of *is* is, it's a pretty safe bet that they will report your mink-lined handcuffs and the wet fettucine as well. And the trapeze in the mirrored bedroom of one of your practice lovers, who will now start selling his story to the *National Enquirer* under the heading "I was her landing pad when Monica *really* swung." Pardon me if I sound a teeny bit bitter.

3. The case will drag on for months, or maybe even years. The publicity will *help* your social life, because anyone having their fifteen minutes of fame[16] will have flashy escorts and be in demand for parties. (For a change, you would be in demand as

---

[16] Andy Warhol said "fifteen minutes," but he didn't look like he was very good with numbers.

a *conversation* piece.) But it will *stop* any chance you have of meeting a really good candidate. What successful married man in public life could risk dating you?

4. Even if you win, *your* lawyers will be there. With their hands out. You will get only a small part of any settlement. There's a reason that lawyers charge more than hookers. They give you a better screwing.

So try to settle privately.

In the **direct cash-in** (I call it Route Gennifer Flowers), you don't get one-time money from your man. You get a steady source of income in the form of a position (a *job* position) and a title, or use him as your ticket to the public. It's like playing Monopoly and always drawing the "Collect $35 card from Community Chest" card.

The first possibility is a cushy job. Your man is in a position to find you a job, either with your company or with one of his friend's companies. Be specific about the job you want. Don't settle for a boring job, or a job without a lot of good male candidates for you, or one that isn't close to shopping, or one away from the right social circle, or one where all the people speak different languages. Try to avoid a job that will require you to do work. Companies have plenty of positions filled by people who push useless paper around, or do nothing but check up on the work that other people produce, or produce reports that no one reads, or otherwise just take up space. That's the kind of job you want. To get to the *really* unproductive jobs, though, you have to go to the public sector: government, charities, foundations, etc. Private-sector organizations usually have stockholders who somehow measure results. Have you ever heard anyone say "It was a good year for the Department of the Interior. They produced 27 ½ more square miles of interior"?

The second possibility is going public. This can lead to paid interviews and to publishing a book. If you do this, be sure that your attitude is of the innocent party, disillusioned by a deceiving man just as you were by the other married men you were with, sympathetic to the wife and children, and no longer in love with the man who took such callous advantage of you. You have to be the injured party. If you come across as scheming, devious, or cold-hearted, America won't watch your interviews or buy your book. Americans demand a lead character who is *likable*. After all, why do you think Bill Cosby adapted a British television show[17] to the U.S. by changing its lead character from a crotchety old man disliked by his neighbors into The Cosby Show II? To make him *likable*. If you say "My man was powerful and I thought he looked sexy so I wangled (that's a real word) my way into his office, flashed him my sexy underwear, told him I had a big crush on him, kissed him, fondled him, performed oral sex on him half a dozen times before I thought to ask whether he knew my name, ignored the effect on his wife and child and co-workers and the people right outside his office, and then he had the nerve to end our relationship," people will say you deserved whatever you got. If you say "*He* noticed *me*, told me how much he liked me, kissed me first, stuck his face into my bosom, exposed himself to me, had me service him while he conducted business on the telephone, inserted objects into me for his pleasure, used his position (his job, I mean) to impress me, told me how unfulfilling his marriage was and that we might be together in a few years, called me for phone sex when he was horny, told me he had hundreds of affairs, and then dumped me and took my job away," people will say that boys will be boys. It's so *unfair*.

---

[17] *One Foot in the Grave*

But I digress. Regardless of the unfairness, you have to play the injured party. You can do this in your interviews and in your book. Don't be scared at the idea of a book. I'm talking of you *producing* a book, not actually *writing* a book. This is a simple process and does not have to involve any writing at all on your part. Here are the steps:

1. Get a flack who is willing to churn out a volume of real sentences, written quickly and edited poorly, based on your public statements and a few hours of conversation with you. It helps if he has already made a reputation by cashing in on public figures.

2. Find a publisher and publish quickly.

3. Promote immediately, to take advantage of the brief interval between your book being published and its consignment to remainder tables.

This should provide enough income for you to cover your basic expenses, get you some expense-paid trips to *interesting* places for book-signings (I imagine that some people in Salt Lake City will buy your book, but they won't get them signed by you!), and garner you enough publicity that you can take your mind off of the long process of re-building your life. Then you can write a guide telling other women how they can follow the trail you have bravely blazed on your knee pads, and start all over again at Stage One.

Quotations

Stage One:
David Stockman, *The Triumph of Politics*, page 45.
guidance counselor: Fran Lebowitz, "Tips for Teens," *Newsweek*, 1/1/79.
Erica Jong in the *Sunday Times Magazine*, quoted in the *South China Morning Post*, 2/12/94

Stage Three:
cup size: *Square Pegs*, CBS-TV, 10/4/82

Stage Four:
Charlie Chaplin in his autobiography, quoted in *Newsweek* 1/9/78

Stage Six:
Greek: Archilocus of Paros
news anchor: The Ted Baxter character on *The Mary Tyler Moore Show*, 1/29/72

Stage Seven:
mistress: Attributed to Walter Winchell in *The Gossip Wars*, Milt Machlin
hearts and minds: Attributed to an American general, in *Nuremburg and Vietnam: An American Tragedy*, Telford Taylor
quality: Mao Tse-Tung, quoted in *Viet Cong*

Monica Lewinsky quotations from *Monica's Story* by Andrew Morton, *Monica Speaks* by Joel Green, and the Starr Report.

Prospect Rating Sheet

Name: ________ Age: ________

Profession: ________________

Current income: ________________

over $200,000: 15 points
over $100,000: 10 points
under $100,000: 0 points

Head shot: [ ]

Income sources:

  Salary: ☐ 0 points
  Bonus: ☐ 5 points
  Stock options: ☐ 10 points if in the money, 5 points if not, 0 points if restricted
  Inherited wealth: ☐ 15 points

[ ]

Prospects: ________________
____
____

Marital status	Quality of wardrobe	Quality of office carpet
single: ☐-20 points	Italian suits: ☐ 10 points	plush: ☐ 5 points
divorced: ☐-25 points	domestic suits: ☐ 5 points	average: ☐ 0 points
married: ☐10 points	leisure suits: ☐ -10 points	knee-scraper: ☐ -2 points
bigamist: ☐15 points	office casual: ☐ 0 points	tile: ☐ -4 points

[ ]

Appearance	"Envy" potential
Gorgeous: ☐ 5 points	Girlfriends will die: ☐ 10 points
Handsome: ☐ 5 points	Girlfriends will turn green: ☐ 8 points
Passable: ☐ 5 points	Girlfriends will turn nauseous: ☐ 0 points
Unacceptable: ☐ -20 points	Girlfriends will ignore: ☐ -20 points

[ ]

Opportunities for contact			
Country club bar	☐ 5 points	At affairs for "fun" charities	☐ 6 points
Athletic club juice bar	☐ 4 points	At affairs for boring charities	☐ 3 points
As a visitor to his work	☐ 2 points	At his swinger's club	☐ 10 points
As an employee at his work	☐ 8 points	Other (assign a point value)	☐

Total Points: [ ]

Prospect Rating Sheet

Name: ____________ Age: ____________
Profession: ____________________

Current income: ____________________
over $200,000: 15 points
over $100,000: 10 points
under $100,000: 0 points

Income sources:
  Salary: ☐ 0 points
  Bonus: ☐ 5 points
  Stock options: ☐ 10 points if in the money, 5 points if not, 0 points if restricted
  Inherited wealth: ☐ 15 points

Head shot:

Prospects: ____
____
____

Marital status	Quality of wardrobe	Quality of office carpet
single: ☐-20 points	Italian suits: ☐ 10 points	plush: ☐ 5 points
divorced: ☐-25 points	domestic suits: ☐ 5 points	average: ☐ 0 points
married: ☐10 points	leisure suits: ☐ -10 points	knee-scraper: ☐ -2 points
bigamist: ☐15 points	office casual: ☐ 0 points	tile: ☐ -4 points

Appearance	"Envy" potential
Gorgeous: ☐ 5 points	Girlfriends will die: ☐ 10 points
Handsome: ☐ 5 points	Girlfriends will turn green: ☐ 8 points
Passable: ☐ 5 points	Girlfriends will turn nauseous: ☐ 0 points
Unacceptable: ☐ -20 points	Girlfriends will ignore: ☐ -20 points

Opportunities for contact			
Country club bar	☐ 5 points	At affairs for "fun" charities	☐ 6 points
Athletic club juice bar	☐ 4 points	At affairs for boring charities	☐ 3 points
As a visitor to his work	☐ 2 points	At his swinger's club	☐ 10 points
As an employee at his work	☐ 8 points	Other (assign a point value)	☐

Total Points:

Prospect Rating Sheet

Name: _________ Age: _________
Profession: ___________________

Current income: ________________
over $200,000: 15 points
over $100,000: 10 points
under $100,000: 0 points

Income sources:
  Salary: ☐ 0 points
  Bonus: ☐ 5 points
  Stock options: ☐ 10 points if in the money, 5 points if not, 0 points if restricted
  Inherited wealth: ☐ 15 points

Head shot:

Prospects: ____
____
____

Marital status	Quality of wardrobe	Quality of office carpet
single: ☐-20 points	Italian suits: ☐ 10 points	plush: ☐ 5 points
divorced: ☐-25 points	domestic suits: ☐ 5 points	average: ☐ 0 points
married: ☐10 points	leisure suits: ☐ -10 points	knee-scraper: ☐ -2 points
bigamist: ☐15 points	office casual: ☐ 0 points	tile: ☐ -4 points

Appearance	"Envy" potential
Gorgeous: ☐ 5 points	Girlfriends will die: ☐ 10 points
Handsome: ☐ 5 points	Girlfriends will turn green: ☐ 8 points
Passable: ☐ 5 points	Girlfriends will turn nauseous: ☐ 0 points
Unacceptable: ☐ -20 points	Girlfriends will ignore: ☐ -20 points

Opportunities for contact			
Country club bar	☐ 5 points	At affairs for "fun" charities	☐ 6 points
Athletic club juice bar	☐ 4 points	At affairs for boring charities	☐ 3 points
As a visitor to his work	☐ 2 points	At his swinger's club	☐ 10 points
As an employee at his work	☐ 8 points	Other (assign a point value)	☐

Total Points:

Contact Record

Name: _______________________
Profession: _______________________
Current position: _______________________
Favorite position: _______________________
Alternate positions: _______________________   _______________________
_______________________   _______________________

Date of first contact: _______________________
Date of first intimate contact: _______________________
Date he first learned your name: _______________________

Phone Sex Log

Date	Time	Duration You Him	Local ?	Long Distance ?	Collect ? (Note 1)	Recorded?

Note 1: Record who paid. Did he use 10-10-321?

Date Log

Date	Type of Date (See Stage Six)	First clothing article unfastened	Grade of climax (Note 1)

Note 1: Enter one of

    10 = wild, shrieking, simultaneous, twice
    9 = wild, shrieking, simultaneous, once
    8 = simultaneous
    7 = you before him
    6 = you after him

    5 = just you
    4 = just him
    3 = just him; he cries "Mommy!"
    2 = not attempted on this date
    1 = just attempted on this date

Pet Name Response

Name you tried	Response score	Name you tried	Response score
"Darling"		"Cupcake"	
"Dear"		"Mr. Frosting"	
"Stud muffin"		"Mr. President"	
"Monster pants"			
"My head man"			

Note: Enter one of:

    5 = driven wild with passion
    4 = laughed and hugged you
    3 = smiled
    2 = looked up
    1 = no response
    0 = grimace

Attach cloth with DNA sample:

Contact Record

Name: _______________________
Profession: _______________________
Current position: _______________________
Favorite position: _______________________
Alternate positions: _______________________   _______________________
_______________________   _______________________

Date of first contact: _______________________
Date of first intimate contact: _______________________
Date he first learned your name: _______________________

Phone Sex Log

Date	Time	Duration You Him	Local ?	Long Distance ?	Collect ? (Note 1)	Recorded?

Note 1: Record who paid. Did he use 10-10-321?

Date Log

Date	Type of Date (See Stage Six)	First clothing article unfastened	Grade of climax (Note 1)

Note 1: Enter one of

10 = wild, shrieking, simultaneous, twice	5 = just you
9 = wild, shrieking, simultaneous, once	4 = just him
8 = simultaneous	3 = just him; he cries "Mommy!"
7 = you before him	2 = not attempted on this date
6 = you after him	1 = just attempted on this date

Pet Name Response

Name you tried	Response score	Name you tried	Response score
"Darling"		"Cupcake"	
"Dear"		"Mr. Frosting"	
"Stud muffin"		"Mr. President"	
"Monster pants"			
"My head man"			

Note: Enter one of:
- 5 = driven wild with passion
- 4 = laughed and hugged you
- 3 = smiled
- 2 = looked up
- 1 = no response
- 0 = grimace

Attach cloth with DNA sample:

Contact Record

Name: _______________________

Profession: _______________________

Current position: _______________________

Favorite position: _______________________

Alternate positions: _______________________   _______________________

_______________________   _______________________

Date of first contact: _______________________

Date of first intimate contact: _______________________

Date he first learned your name: _______________________

Phone Sex Log

Date	Time	Duration You Him		Local ?	Long Distance ?	Collect ? (Note 1)	Recorded?

Note 1: Record who paid. Did he use 10-10-321?

Date Log

Date	Type of Date (See Stage Six)	First clothing article unfastened	Grade of climax (Note 1)

Note 1: Enter one of

10 = wild, shrieking, simultaneous, twice   5 = just you

9 = wild, shrieking, simultaneous, once   4 = just him

8 = simultaneous   3 = just him; he cries "Mommy!"

7 = you before him   2 = not attempted on this date

6 = you after him   1 = just attempted on this date

Pet Name Response

Name you tried	Response score	Name you tried	Response score
"Darling"		"Cupcake"	
"Dear"		"Mr. Frosting"	
"Stud muffin"		"Mr. President"	
"Monster pants"			
"My head man"			

Note: Enter one of:

5 = driven wild with passion

4 = laughed and hugged you

3 = smiled

2 = looked up

1 = no response

0 = grimace

Attach cloth with DNA sample:

Gift Register

To/From: _____________________

His personal data

Shirt size:	neck: ______	sleeve: ______			
Trousers:	waist: ______	leg: ______	inside leg: ______	snug fit: ______	
Jacket:	size: ______	S/M/R/L: ______			
Fabric:	silk: ______	cotton: ______	wool: ______	hair: ______	

Color preference (items that show): __________________

Color preference (items that don't show): ______________

Gifts given

Gift	Description (Note 1)	Date	Remarks (Note 2)

Note 1: color, inscription, monogram, etc.
Note 2: did he refer to it, wear it in public, use it instead of a gift from his wife, etc.

Gifts Received

Gift	Description	Date	Reason (Note 1)	Wardrobe (Note 2)	Quality (Note 3)	Estimated Cost

Note 1: Enter one of
    Birthday   Valentine's   Christmas/Hanukkah
    Anniversary   Special sexual act   Other

Note 2: If clothing, note whether it is stored with the
    "ultra-thin just-before-wedding-pictures" wardrobe   "chunky" wardrobe
    "thin" wardrobe   "retaining water" wardrobe
    "normal" wardrobe   "post-binge-weekend" wardrobe

Note 3: Enter one of
    A (thoughtful, expensive, a size too small)   D (not thoughtful, inexpensive, a size too large)
    B (thoughtful, expensive, the right size)   E (provided by his company*)
    C (thoughtful, inexpensive, the right size)   F (gift with company logo)
                 * expensive items provided with funds from a charity rate "B" or higher

Gift Register

To/From: ___________________

His personal data

    Shirt size: neck: ______   sleeve: ______

    Trousers: waist: ______   leg: ______   inside leg: ______   snug fit: ______

    Jacket: size: ______   S/M/R/L: ______

    Fabric: silk: ______   cotton: ______   wool: ______   hair: ______

    Color preference (items that show): ___________________

    Color preference (items that don't show): ___________________

Gifts given

Gift	Description (Note 1)	Date	Remarks (Note 2)

Note 1: color, inscription, monogram, etc.
Note 2: did he refer to it, wear it in public, use it instead of a gift from his wife, etc.

Gifts Received

Gift	Description	Date	Reason (Note 1)	Wardrobe (Note 2)	Quality (Note 3)	Estimated Cost

Note 1: Enter one of   Birthday   Valentine's   Christmas/Hanukkah
    Anniversary   Special sexual act   Other

Note 2: If clothing, note whether it is stored with the
    "ultra-thin just-before-wedding-pictures" wardrobe   "chunky" wardrobe
    "thin" wardrobe   "retaining water" wardrobe
    "normal" wardrobe   "post-binge-weekend" wardrobe

Note 3: Enter one of
    A (thoughtful, expensive, a size too small)   D (not thoughtful, inexpensive, a size too large)
    B (thoughtful, expensive, the right size)   E (provided by his company*)
    C (thoughtful, inexpensive, the right size)   F (gift with company logo)
    * expensive items provided with funds from a charity rate "B" or higher

Gift Register

To/From: _____________________

His personal data

Shirt size: neck: ______   sleeve: ______

Trousers: waist: ______   leg: ______   inside leg: ______   snug fit: ______

Jacket: size: ______   S/M/R/L: ______

Fabric: silk: ______   cotton: ______   wool: ______   hair: ______

Color preference (items that show): ___________________

Color preference (items that don't show): ______________

Gifts given

Gift	Description (Note 1)	Date	Remarks (Note 2)

Note 1: color, inscription, monogram, etc.
Note 2: did he refer to it, wear it in public, use it instead of a gift from his wife, etc.

Gifts Received

Gift	Description	Date	Reason (Note 1)	Wardrobe (Note 2)	Quality (Note 3)	Estimated Cost

Note 1: Enter one of   Birthday   Valentine's   Christmas/Hanukkah
    Anniversary   Special sexual act   Other

Note 2: If clothing, note whether it is stored with the
    "ultra-thin just-before-wedding-pictures" wardrobe   "chunky" wardrobe
    "thin" wardrobe   "retaining water" wardrobe
    "normal" wardrobe   "post-binge-weekend" wardrobe

Note 3: Enter one of
    A (thoughtful, expensive, a size too small)   D (not thoughtful, inexpensive, a size too large)
    B (thoughtful, expensive, the right size)   E (provided by his company*)
    C (thoughtful, inexpensive, the right size)   F (gift with company logo)
    * expensive items provided with funds from a charity rate "B" or higher